SHATTERED PIECES

Iesha S. Bryant

DEDICATION

I would like to dedicate this book in loving memory of Evangelist Caroline Bobbitt Johnson (My Gram). She has been a true inspiration to me. She's been a woman of many hats in the family and what better way to honor her than through my very own first book. My gram departed her life April 2021, which has been a challenging month for me. I was diagnosed with covid on April 12, 2021 and had to quarantine for fourteen days. Two days into quarantine, I received a disturbing phone call from my mother (Wilma Bryant) that shattered my entire life. She broke the news to me that my gram had passed away. My heart fell to the ground and I did not know what to do since I could not leave the house. All I could tell myself was that no way that could have been true. As time passed and days went by alone in the house, mind wondering, body aching, all I could do was just cry. On April 22, 2021, I called my mother to tell her that I received a negative covid result and she said hurry home because gram was going to be buried on April 24, 2021. As I approached my gram house in Enfield NC, I began to feel anxious of the unknown. That moment I walked into her house and realized that her home was empty. I fell to my knees and could not believe that my gram had left me in this world alone. That day I lost part of me and I knew that my life was not going to be the same. So, I made a vow to myself that when I published my first poetry book whether it was going to be near her birthday (February 20th) or Mother's Day, it was going to be all about her. Poetry was my way of coping with the pain. So, here is my first book, my gram. Happy Heavenly birthday and Mother's Day. I love you and you will forever be in my heart!

TABLE OF CONTENT

A HUMBLE MELODY

A voice so faint and sweet.
A voice well put together is so neat!

A voice that can touch any heart.
Whether you're here, there or far apart.

A voice that lights anyone's day.
Knows what to say.
Has the right words to make everything ok!

A voice that can heal.
Light any heart with such a thrill.

Whether you're up or down,
Just the sound of such a lovely voice will turn any
Frown upside down.

A voice like a melody,
like two birds singing and harmonizing,
that will fulfill any heart like it does to mine.

A voice I would give up anything to hear,
A voice that I would cherish and hold so dear.

A voice that lights my day, puts a smile on my face,
A melody to my heart and guides my family.
My love, my heart, the voice I love is my gram!

COMFORT

A love for a grandmother is rare to find,
A love for a grandmother should be special like mine.

She hold secrets when we vent to her,
She is always there when we go see her.

She spoils us, cooks our favorite food even when she is
tired, she never complains.
She taught us right from wrong, taught us how to pray
and get along.

She never took sides when things went left between us,
She made things fair by letting us talk it out before she
grabbed that belt.

We know we had to get right by the look on her face,
Grandma always said "I don't play!"

Everywhere grandma went we were right there, from the
grocery store to the laundromat, to church, we were
there.

She never lost sight of us.
She was our protector, our provider, she was our shield.

We took the best naps when we were done playing,
so comfortable, so soothing.
We would wake up and she was praying.

How we miss the days when we were young.
There was no other place that we would want to be other
than at grandmas'.

HOUSE OF LOVE

Grandma's house was the place to be.
It was the place to set our minds free.
We laugh, we joke, and we talk about our life.
Everything we've been through with all the sacrifice.

Who could guess this big and tall house,
can have so much love and care.
No matter where you go,
Grandma's house was a place nowhere else could
compare.

The warmth feeling that you gain,
Is the feeling that takes away all your pain.
The burst of energy and love that arouses is the feeling
we get from Grandma's house.

MY LEADER

Sundays was the best day at grandma's house,
We all knew when we stayed with her,
church was where we would be.
It was like a routine how everything used to be,
My gram would get up, cook breakfast and iron our
clothes on top of the heater.

"Get dressed and do not make me late" she would
always say.
I knew right then I had to hurry up and clean my plate.
I paid attention to everything she did,
I wanted to learn and be just like her.
She was someone I looked up to,
She was my leader as a kid.

Down the road we would go, in her green Nissan was
always fun.
We would sing and laugh together, that was our bond.
As we arrived at church, she would always park near the
road beside that light pole.
All you could hear was people singing and shouting,
As we walked inside everything got louder.
I knew exactly where we were headed, straight to the
second row,
That was my gram's favorite spot.

From broadcasting, to preaching, to singing and
shouting,
Those were her hobbies everyday it showed.
She knew exactly what to say to keep the church stirred.
It made me happy to watch her, to learn from her,
To see that smile on her face.
I realized right then, that church was her favorite place.

SHE WAS THERE!

Growing up as a child, my grandmother was always
there,
She never missed an event, not even grandparents day at
school.
When she came around,
She always knew how to brighten my day.
She was everything to me,
She was my precious jewel.

My gram was never too busy for me,
I could call her all day and all night,
She always answered with care,
No matter what occurred my grandmother was always
there!

She's an example of a promise to keep,
I know without her my heart would skip a beat.
So I made a promise to always praise her while she is
here on this earth.
To spoil her and give her the flowers she deserve,
Because my grandmother, my gram did the same for me.

We was like a pair that could not be taken apart,
Confused and lost I would be if she was to be taken
from my heart.

As I got older, I understood what it means to love and to
care,
That is what my grandmother showed and drilled in me,
Her promise that she would always be right there!

GO ON!

I remember like it was yesterday,
My first year in college, freshman orientation,
Nervous but yet exciting,
Walking into the cafeteria and there she was,
My gram and mom sitting at the buffet table,
Smiling so bright.

They looked so proud as I walked in,
Heart saddened to know off to school I had to go.
"Esha, you are a smart girl" those are the words I cannot
forget.
Those are the words that made me who I am,
Those are the words that brought me this far.

My gram always knew what to say to boost my
confidence,
I could always count on her for a compliment.
My gram told me no matter what happens in life,
to always go on,
because God is still in charge.

ON EDGE

When I got that call that you were sick and had to go to
the hospital,
I was on edge.

My mind started racing not knowing what to think or
how to feel,
I was on edge.

I called almost every hour just to see how you were
doing.
Mom would say,
"She is fine, she is eating and watching tv,"
I heard your voice. I took a breath.
I exhaled.

"She has to stay a couple more days", the doctor stated,
Do I need to come stay with her?
Do I need to take off?
Again,
I was back on edge.
"Go to work, she is alright", my mom said.

My family knows when it comes to my Gram,
any little thing puts me on edge.

They have to be cautious about what they say to me.
They know my Gram is my heartbeat.

Every waking day I would pray,
Lord, please touch my grandmother's body as she lay in
that hospital bed.
Never seen my grandmother in the hospital,
never seen her sick to the point she has to remain in bed.
This is all new,
What is going on?
I'm trying not to worry but I can not help but to be on
edge.

Dear lord, whatever that is over my grandmother's body
let it pass through.
This mind of mine would not let me be calm, I do not
know what to do.
I was on edge.
Alone, she must feels, not knowing where she is at or
whose around,
Not knowing what to do or what to say, there are no
familiar faces.
This pandemic got everyone going crazy.

You can't do this, can't do that.
You can't even visit some places.

Two weeks they say, here I am counting down the days.
I pray everyday, lord watch over my Gram, I hope they
keep her safe.

In places like that rehab center you are in, I heard
stories.
I heard what people say.

Lord heal my Gram so she can come home,
It's her voice and face I can't go without everyday.

Alone, she must feel in there with no familiar faces,
I do not know all what the world is coming to during
this pandemic,
I just wish it comes to a close and to an end.
It has caused so many broken hearts that I don't think no
one but God can mend.

BROKEN PIECES!

April 14th, a day I will never forget.
The day my heart dropped and my life fell apart.
The day I received that call.
It was the second day of quarantine.
Already tired, already weak, slowly,
everything was beginning to fall.

Gram passed away!
"Stop playing!" was my response to it all.
Lost and confused!
Nowhere to go, nowhere to run to.
The day I didn't know what to do.
I buried myself under my covers,
yelling and screaming,
Lord, could all this be a dream?
Did my gram really leave me?
Alone and sick with eight days left in this house,
not knowing what to do or how to cope.
I don't even know if it's real.
How am I supposed to feel?

I prayed and prayed that it was all just a dream,
I can't swallow this big pill.
My mind racing and hard pounding,
I made a video call just to see,
right before my eyes,

my Gram lay lifeless in her bed.
My whole life shattered.

I broke down and cried.
My whole heart was right there in her bed.
This image, I would never get out of my head.

CONFUSED

As time passed and days went by,
Alone I lay weak in my bed.

Not knowing what to do, but cry!
"Focus and get your health right," they say.
Soon you can be with your family instead.

How can I find the strength to do so,
When everything was racing in my head.

Each passing day since I got the news,
I try to piece together what was said.
I can't believe my grandmother passed away,
I'm never going to be more than just okay.
My world was spinning, I felt so confused.

WHAT HAPPENED TO THE DAYS?

I miss the days we all use to be at your house,
The excitement of getting up packing our bags to getting
on the road.
I already knew when we arrived you would be standing
there waiting at the door.
Seeing your face always brightened my day.
Waking up and you standing there at the stove,
Sweet smell of bacon, table full of pancakes,
breakfast at grandma's house was always good for our
soul.
Oh, how i missed the good times, what happened to the
days?

The days we all would run and play outside for hours,
From basketball, to hopscotch, to jump rope, to falling
in the leaves.
I miss the days you would sit on the porch and watch us
so we wouldn't mess up your flowers or scar our knees.
Oh, how time flies, what happened to the days?

The days when we always had something to do,
We had books to read, plenty of games to play and you
even made laundry fun because we got to hang clothes
on the line with you.
There was never a dull moment, never had a bad day, we
barely even got in your way.

Oh, how I miss the fun we shared with you.
My gram, what happened to those days?

EMPTY!

Grandma ! Grandma ! Lord,what am I going to do?
My heart has left me so empty and all alone,
Grandma you meant everything to me.
You were my smile, my joy, my laughter, it all came
from you!
You made me who I am today.
Everything I have accomplished was all for you.
Grandma you were my world!
I feel so shattered and empty without you!
Lord, what am I going to do?

Every minute in between classes and breaks at work we
was always on the phone,
Your voice was my comfort when I've had a long and
rough day.
"Hi, my iesha"
That was all I needed to put a smile on my face.
When I needed a getaway or a visit home everyone
knew,
It was you, I would run too.
Grandma ! Grandma ! I am going to miss you so much !
I feel so lost without you.
Lord, what am I going to do?
Grandma, I need you !

HAPPY HEAVENLY BIRTHDAY!

February 20th, a date I will never forget,
Happy Heavenly Birthday Gram!
In our hearts you will forever remain,
82 years on earth, God thank you for sending us this
woman in our life,
All she has done will never go in vain.

She taught us a lot of things like to stand up and be bold,
To always treat people kind,
I'm going to miss all the songs we sang.
Those were the good times.
I love you gram I wish I could turn back the hands of
time.
We will continue to cherish the memories we shared,
We will keep them in our hearts.
Forever you will remain.
You were everything to us, you were one of a kind,
Happy birthday my gram!
Lord, I'm trying to keep from crying.

ONE MORE TIME

Hi! my gram,
Hi! My Iesha!
That was our thing, that's how we would greet each
other.
Oh, what I would do to pick up the phone to hear it one
more time.
It would make my day,
It would make my heart sing to hear my gram voice
once again.

I MISS YOU GRAM!

My gram, I miss you oh so much,
There's not a day that goes by that I don't think of you.
I try not to cry,
What am I supposed to do when my heart is aching
and broken into pieces?
Gram I miss you!
I try to remain strong,
I know crying is something you would not want me to
do.
What am I supposed to do when everyday I have to live
on without you?
Not being able to talk to you, see you and hug you,
My mind been so cloudy and confused ever since the
day I lost you,
Gram, I miss you!

HER SIGNATURE

My gram always had a thing for hats,
Hats was her signature.
She had them in all different shapes and colors.
She never left the house without one,
Everytime we go out shopping, she's always buying
another,
My grandmother loved her hats, that was her signature.

My mind would often take me back to when I lost her,
Never knew if it was true or whether it was a joke,
All I knew when I got to her house, it was empty where
she sat.
My mom called and told me to meet her at the church,
When I arrived it was a lot different folks.
Heart racing, knees getting weak and mind going in
circles,
When I walked in and turned that corner,
There she was, my gram, lying there in the casket in her
white hat.

My heart fell and my soul cried out,
How can I get my gram back?
She can't leave me.
I can not believe it was her lying right there,
body so cold all wrapped up in white.
It was the hat that made it real,

The pain hit so hard, it felt like a knife.
My gram you told me you would always be there,
This is one pain I can't fight!

My gram, take your rest.
You will forever be missed
Thank you, job well done.

You speak, I listen.
Christway Holiness was home,
Your footprints remain.

HER PRAYER

As I lay down at night, I can often hear my gram
praying,
Faintly and clear, as if she was laying directly beside
me.
As I close my eyes to drift off to sleep,
All I can hear,
"Father God in the name of Jesus,
Lord we come to you as humble as we know how,
In our hearts just thanking you Lord,
How you spared our life so many times."
Distant but yet clear,
It was her voice, I could hear in my head.
My gram was a praying woman and always taught us
that there is power in prayer.
Until this day, I can still hear her praying inside my
head.

ABOUT THE AUTHOR

Iesha S. Bryant is currently a certified Correctional Officer with a dream of becoming an acclaimed poet. She was born in Rocky Mount, NC and raised in the small town of Enfield, NC by her mother Wilma Bryant. She always had a passion for helping others and the true definition of a "people person". Iesha was the quiet, down to earth individual who never met a stranger. She was trained at North Carolina Central University where she earned her Master's degree specializing in criminal justice. Iesha was a reader, daydreamer and often spent the majority of her time writing. Fueled by a lifelong passion for poetry, she has written numerous unpublished poems in her spare time on a variety of topics of which will soon be published.